What people are saying about

"GOD SAYS WHEN!"

and

TC Bradley

There is but one message I really hope you gain from reading "God Says When" and that is God, my friend, is in total control! You do not control your destiny. You do not call the shots. GOD SAYS WHEN!

You are reading this book for a reason. You may not quite understand what it has to do with your life, but God has your plans laid out for you.

We are not promised a tomorrow. We will stand in front of God one day and we will be held accountable for how we lived our lives.

TC Bradley's ordeal affected more than just him. God put into play a message that needs to be heard by a multitude of people... people like me, who thought that they were in control.

God needed me to hear this simple phrase... GOD SAYS WHEN!

R. Michael Parker
CEO and Founder of Aboutabiz.com/ LexiPays.com and Advantage Media SEO

Having known TC Bradley for years, not just as a leader in a national real estate community, but as a trusted friend as well; I was touched and inspired by what I came to learn happened that night.

It was rare that we ever had a conversation where we didn't examine the spiritual side of an issue and how God has touched our lives or the lives of people we work with in some way. We would examine why this or that was happening and marvel at his presence in our lives. I'm blessed that God says when, and my friend is still with me.

John Alexander
www.johnalexanderblog.com

God Says When!

TC Bradley

Dedication

George F. Bradley, my father, who stood for me when I could not stand for myself. I love and miss you, Dad.

Mary Ann Bradley, my precious mother who taught me to trust the Lord always. No matter what. Oh, Mom, you just don't know how much I love and miss you.

Vickie Bradley, my beautiful wife who saved my life in more ways than one. Peas and carrots forever! I love you Sweetheart!

Renee M. Blissett, my baby sister, who got up and prayed for me at 2 am in the morning. Thanks Sis and I love you!

Jayden, Dionis and Alexandria, my precious grandsons and granddaughter, your grandpa loves you!

Laurinda and Jose, Kevin and Eleni and Nicole, I love each of you more than you will ever know.

Midge Falin, my precious aunt who prayed for me and reminded me that's just what family does.

Rev. Dan Bradley, my uncle, who had his own "God Says When" moment and still found time to pray for me.

Pastor Dan Willis, not only the only man I call "Pastor" but the man who taught me how to pray and to be a Christian man. I learned more from your faithful walk than any sermon you ever preached. You are not only my pastor but my brother and I love you.

Christine Hamric, thank you for your friendship and for putting your "heart prints" on everything that you do for me. You never cease to amaze me with your gifts.

Stephen J. Young, thanks Doc for always being there and for giving me the title of this book that will touch all nations!

My VIP partners, JL Ferren, Chuck Fowler, Big Dave Entenman, Kasey Hasko, Lois and Kristie Kral, Carlos Agosto, Marc Vaughan, Dr. Sam Galati, Jim "JT" Toolen, Lady Edna, Susan Jones and Steven C. Johnson, I thank you for standing with Vickie and me in our darkest hour.

Dr. Conrad and the entire nursing staff at HealthPark: Thank You! Thank You! Thank You!

And finally, Paramedic Raymond Weigand, because of your heroic efforts that morning and your refusal to give up on me, even when it looked like all hope was gone, I am here today. You are one of my heroes and I am forever grateful.

FOREWORD

My name is Raymond J. Wiegand. I am a Paramedic with Lee County EMS.

At 2:16 AM on the morning of March 21, 2012 I was dispatched to a chest pain patient in south Cape Coral.

I arrived on scene to find a middle age male lying in bed in a first floor bedroom.

He told me he was awakened from sleep with chest and left arm pain and became very short of breath when he tried to walk downstairs.

In Paramedic school they teach you how patients present symptoms.

Mr. Bradley was a textbook presentation of someone having a heart attack.

After completing my assessment and performing a 12 lead EKG, I informed Mr. Bradley that I believed he was having a heart attack.

I explained to him the tests we do in the field are not conclusive.

He needed to be evaluated at the ER and blood work completed for a diagnosis.

He began to express his concern about the cost. He informed me he was starting to feel better and didn't think he needed to go.

My gut feeling told me differently.

After several minutes of trying to decide whether he would refuse treatment or be transported, I explained that "time is muscle".

The longer he waited, the more damage was occurring to his heart, and his wife was becoming more upset, as well.

She asked him, *"Do you want to live or die?"*

This must have struck a chord as he decided to go and he moved to the stretcher.

Things were progressing like most other "Chest Pain" calls.

Per our treatment protocol, I gave him Aspirin and Nitroglycerine, thanked the Cape Coral Firefighters for their help and cleared them from the call.

As I placed a tourniquet on his arm and began feeling for a vein to place an IV, he turned to me and said, *"I feel funny."*

The paramedic in me was about to say, "Sir, can you describe funny?" but I never got the chance.

Suddenly his eyes rolled back into his head and he became unresponsive.

Mr. Bradley went into a cardiac arrhythmia identified as ventricular fibrillation.

My partner and I began CPR and defibrillated him twice.

Shortly after the second defibrillation and resuming chest compressions, he began to open his eyes and then asked, *"What happened?"*

I couldn't believe he woke up after going into cardiac arrest right in front of me!

The fire department returned to the scene and accompanied the patient and me to the hospital.

> *I continually reflect on that minute and thirty seconds when Mr. Bradley was clinically dead.*

I think about the procedures I performed, the medications I gave, and the two shocks I delivered.

I'm in awe that I was able to get it all accomplished in such a short time and, remarkably, that the treatment worked just as it should.

When he woke up he was surprised to hear what had just happened but not nearly as astounded as me.

I informed him that he was a statistic.

He was one of the few to survive an out-of-hospital sudden cardiac arrest.

Three days later I found out what, for me, is one of the hardest parts of being a paramedic.

After transporting another patient to HealthPark ER, I went to Mr. Bradley's room to see how he was.

That's when it happened.

All he had to say was two words, "Thank You."

Hearing him say that caused me to choke up and fight back tears.

I had to cut our conversation short to keep my composure and headed back to the ambulance.

On May 24, 2012 I had the pleasure of being reunited with Mr. Bradley and his wife.

They attended our annual EMS Week BBQ at Lakes Park in Fort Myers.

During award presentations Chief Tuttle asked that we both come to the front.

Mr. Bradley shared his story with my co-workers and other attendees.

He also shared another personal note, that this day was also their wedding anniversary.

He thanked me for allowing them to share another anniversary together.

Mr. Bradley then presented me with the Phoenix Award for saving his life.

A Phoenix Award is awarded when an EMS crew treats a patient who is in full cardiac or respiratory arrest (not breathing and/or no pulse).

The patient is treated, often with defibrillation, cardiac drugs and advanced airway procedures and transported to a hospital.

To be counted as a "save" the patient must then recover and be released from the hospital.

This entire incident has been such an amazing experience.

It has allowed me to see the real difference I make in people's lives each and every day.

From that point on I realized that I had a new lifelong friend.

Raymond J. Wiegand
Paramedic
Lee County, Florida

TC Bradley and Raymond G. Weigand

INTRODUCTION

On March 20, 2012, my life was forever changed when at 48 years of age I went into sudden cardiac arrest and was clinically dead for 1.5 to 2 minutes.

Not from the brink of death, but from absolute clinical death with no pulse or heartbeat for 1.5 to 2 minutes.

Most of the people who work on an ambulance will tell you that there is no hope statistically speaking after 1 minute let alone 1.5 to 2 minutes.

My heart had gone into ventricular fibrillation and the paramedics had to shock me 2 times along with chest compressions to get my heartbeat and pulse back.

Out-of-hospital sudden cardiac arrest survival rates are a mere 1%.

The fact that I came back whole without any brain damage, speech damage or paralysis of any kind is also a miracle.

God was not done that day working miracles on my behalf because, when I got to the hospital, it turned out that I had a 100% blockage of my left ascending artery. This condition is referred to as the "Widow Maker" because so few people manage to survive it.

It actually kills 90% of those that it strikes and, of the remaining 10% who survive, 5% have some form of brain damage.

You could say that the odds of my survival were not good at all, yet I survived in spite of overwhelming odds.

The odds were against me but God was for me and gave me three miracles that morning.

I am truly a miracle and I know it.

If you thought that this was a medical story you would be wrong.

I knew when I was recovering in the ICU that God had spared my life for a reason and God slowly unfolded those reasons to my heart and spirit in those days as I lay recovering in my ICU room.

I knew I had a story that people needed to hear and it was clear that my story was NOT a medical story but a FAITH story.

You see, I really was dead but now I am alive and that is a miracle.

People are skeptical that miracles even happen today and, to be quite honest, can you blame them?

We are bombarded on a daily basis with so much negative news that we have become hardened or jaded to the point that we are blind to the miracles that happen every day all around us!

One thing I can share with you right up front is that there are no "coincidences".

None.

If you are reading these words I can promise you that you are not doing so by accident.

You are here by what I like to call "Divine Appointment".

Whether you or someone you love has a dire medical issue, or you have fallen victim to this brutal economy and don't know what to do next, or you feel like giving up because life has not been fair to you -- this much I can tell you with no doubt in my heart: It Ain't Over till it's REALLY Over and God Says When!

It only takes one touch from God to change any situation in a moment!

In a moment God can touch any situation, regardless of how unfavorable or desperate it may be, and things can turn around for you.

As long as you have breath in your body there is hope. As matter of fact, as it was in my case, even when there was <u>no</u> breath in my body there was hope.

If God can reach into that ambulance as I there at 2:00 AM and breathe LIFE into my dead body, he can work a miracle for you, too!

It is never too late for a miracle.

Never.

TC Bradley

WHERE MY STORY STARTS...

My story didn't actually begin on March 20, 2012, when I had my cardiac event. It literally began at the beginning – almost from birth – in the city of Chicago.

You see, it was my earliest childhood experience that forged and directed the decisions I ultimately made that day on March 20.

I was born with a major speech impediment that left me unable to talk like normal children.

I simply could not enunciate words clearly.

My father and mother took me from specialist to specialist in an attempt to correct my condition.

One doctor told my father that I was mentally challenged and that there was no hope for me.

Another doctor told my father that I was deaf and to put me in a special school.

My father refused to accept any of those diagnoses or solutions.

Instead he said, "My son is NOT mentally challenged, he is NOT deaf and I will find someone in Chicago who can fix him. He will live a normal life!"

Now, my father was no stranger to dealing with doctors.

After my brother and I were born he worked in a manufacturing plant in Chicago, where he had a terrible accident that crushed his foot.

His foot was virtually mangled. The doctors wanted to amputate his foot because the injury was so severe.

My father refused, saying, "I have two babies at home to feed. How could I ever provide for them if I am a cripple with one foot?"

So he rejected their advice to cut off his foot.

They warned him that infection could set in and cost him his entire leg and possibly his life, but my father was adamant. He refused to budge on his decision.

Not only did he decline the amputation but he proceeded to check himself out of the hospital that very same night and he headed for home.

He showed up at work the next night for his shift. His job required him to be on his feet the entire time, but he made it through. At the end of his shift, my dad had to literally crawl to the parking lot to climb into his car.

This was in the 1960's, long before the 1-800-Attorney commercials were on the air.

It was the love of his family and unwavering commitment to provide for us (at any cost) that drove my father back to work that next night. All the while he was hurting so badly that he had to again crawl to his car at the end of his shift – only to be followed out by his shift supervisor who fired him on the spot "for being a cripple".

The supervisor made it obvious to everyone around that he was greatly amused watching my father crawl to his car and that he enjoyed "firing the cripple".

True story. Nothing embellished.

My father never did lose that foot. I must add that my father, who was a big man, did eventually cross paths with that supervisor. It was years later. Let's just say that it was not one of that man's favorite days.

So, this was the man to whom the so-called "experts" pronounced his son deaf or mentally challenged.

Good luck with that!

My father and mother finally did find a doctor who could, and did, fix me.

Turns out I had a sub-mucous cleft palate which was repaired with surgery.

I then had to endure speech therapy until I was in the fourth grade because I had to learn how to talk.

Naturally, the kids made fun of me at school. I vividly recall arriving home after my first day of kindergarten. I was crying and, in my faltering speech that only my parents could translate, I informed them that I was never going back again. My father marched me into the back yard and "motivated and inspired" me to return to school.

Which I did.

Fast forward to my last day of high school. I was selected by my class to give the graduation speech and I was honored with a standing ovation by my peers.

My first day of school I was made fun of because I couldn't talk, and my last day of high school I got a standing ovation.

To this day, almost 30-plus years later, my friends remember and talk to me about that speech.

Only God can do something like that. God, through a dad who refused to accept anything less than what he wanted to hear.

Isn't it amazing what can happen if we simply refuse to accept what we do not want?

How different things might have been for me had my father folded under the pressure and accepted what the so-called "experts" had to say.

Let me be <u>crystal</u> <u>clear</u> with you.

Just because an expert has told you something does not mean that they have the final say in the matter.

I have tremendous respect for the medical community, but they are not God and they do not get the final say.

God Says When...Not Man.

Regardless of how hopeless you think your situation is, it ain't over till it's REALLY over.

As long as you have breath in your body you have hope unless you settle or fold your cards.

Never give up and never settle and, whatever you do, don't listen to anyone who tells you that you must be "realistic" or that you are not being "realistic".

"Realistic" is code for settling for less...

Was it realistic for me to be revived and come back without spot or blemish after being without a pulse or heartbeat for 1.5 to 2 minutes?

God has not called his people to be "realistic!"

Was it realistic for me to survive one of the most deadly artery blockages ever, one so deadly that they refer to it as the Widow Maker?

Don't come talking to me about being "realistic" … okay, you're too late!

Brian Wills was 22 years old when he was diagnosed with one of the deadliest and one of the fastest-growing cancers known as Burkitt's Lymphoma.

Incredibly, this rare tumor grew from the size of a golf ball to nine inches in only three days. This is an exceptionally fast-growing cancer that has been known to kill children in a day.

The doctors told him that they didn't believe there was anything they could do for him. That he was too far gone.

They gave him 10 hours to live.

10 Hours to Live!

It was his mother's words that gave him life.

"God's word says that by Jesus' stripes, Brian is healed. Let God be true, and every man a liar!"

Brain completely recovered not only from one of the fastest-growing cancers on the planet, but he also survived the experimental drugs that were administered to him and the other so-called "hopeless cases". The experimental drugs they gave a test group for the most part killed everyone in the group – except Brian.

You can actually pick up Brian's book, *"10 Hours to Live"*, and read his incredibly miraculous story.

I hope you will.

To me, Brian's defining moment in life was when his mother took a stand for her son. She refused to accept what the experts had to say when the doctors came into that hospital room and told her there was no hope and that her son had 10 hours to live.

For me, without question, one of my first defining moments was when my father took a stand for me. He refused to accept what the experts told him, that I was deaf or mentally retarded and would never live a normal life.

Parents, please do not take for granted the authority that God has given you as a mother or father.

You have more power than you know.

It's important to me that you know this part of my story so that the other part makes sense to you.

I was not born "normal", nor was I or have I ever been "normal."

My dreams and goals of what I want to accomplish and achieve are not normal.

I do not hang out with people who encourage me to be "realistic."

I do not go with the "status quo" and, if the herd is running in one direction, it is pretty much a given you will find me leading the charge the other direction.

And now you have a pretty good idea why.

I have embraced this mindset and way of being my entire life and I certainly had it with me on the night of my cardiac arrest.

One of the questions that I get asked is, "Did you have any warning signs that something was wrong with you before the night you went into cardiac arrest?" The answer is yes I did, and I talk about that in the next chapter.

3 WEEKS PRIOR

One of the things that Vickie and I love to do is what we call a "Prosperity Walk" with Lexus, our dog, at a beautiful resort marina here in Cape Coral called Tarpon Point.

I have always been a firm believer in immersing yourself and breathing in places that have what I call atmospheres of wealth and success. Tarpon Point with its million dollar homes and the beautiful yachts parked in the marina certainly provide that atmosphere.

It is a great way to decompress and unwind and we really enjoy walking along the marina checking out the various yachts.

It is a beautiful resort and Vickie and I and Lexus love taking our "Prosperity Walks" there as often as we can.

About three weeks prior to my sudden cardiac arrest, we had just started our "Prosperity walk" when almost immediately I noticed a <u>dramatic</u> change in my body.

I immediately had shortness of breath and an overall uneasy feeling which I had never had before.

I actually felt like I could die at any moment.

Thankfully, there was a chair along the walkway and I was able to sit down, rest and catch my breath.

It was at that moment in time that I KNEW I had crossed a bridge with my body and my health, and that something was terribly wrong with my body.

I told Vickie that I was not feeling well and that we had to cut the walk short. She drove us home where I immediately laid down and rested until whatever was bothering me had passed.

Although I knew something was terribly wrong with my health, I continued to be relentless in running my business.

Working all night in my home-based office was commonplace for me.

I have always taken great pride in the fact that no one can outwork me because I am, and have always been, willing to pay the price necessary for success.

So it was about three weeks before my cardiac event during our "Prosperity Walk" that I knew my body was in crisis – that something was indeed wrong with me.

Instead of slowing me down, this caused me to work even harder.

I feverishly worked on our business pulling back-to-back all-nighters for two weeks in a row.

It was insane the amount of hours that I was working on our business projects.

I literally had no "off" switch.

I remember saying out loud that *"I would be willing to die"* but nothing would stop me from working.

And I meant it.

In hindsight, that was one of the most foolish statements that I could have ever made.

Our word becomes law.

No exceptions.

We frame our world with our words that we speak and what I really meant to do was to draw a line in the sand and let the universe know that I was not going to let a little health issue stop me from working.

> # Instead, I had cast a death sentence on my own life with my own words...

This is one of the reasons that I shared my Father's story at the beginning of this book.

The example he set for me was clear cut.

When his foot was mangled in that accident and they wanted to amputate it, he refused, checked out of the hospital and went to work the next night.

When he had a heart attack, it was only a few months before he was back on the job driving a semi-truck and physically unloading his semi-trailer at his deliveries.

I think one week he had delivered and unloaded 180,000 pounds of freight –months after having his heart attack.

I remember he always had a bottle of Nitroglycerine tablets in his shirt pocket and would go through a bottle a week.

To put that into perspective, when I left the hospital after my heart attack they gave me a prescription for Nitroglycerine with the instructions to take one tablet if I had chest pains and, if I still had chest pains, to take another one and immediately call 911 and get to the hospital.

My Dad was going through a bottle of Nitroglycerine weekly.

Now, on the other side of my own heart attack, I have a new level of respect for what my dad had gone through.

I asked my Aunt Midge, "How was my dad able to do what he did?"

"Your dad found the strength to do what he did through God and love for his family. His family was his life." That was her candid response.

The influence that a father has on his child cannot be understated.

My father's example was firmly ingrained into my very being.

My dad was literally Superman who had overcome any medical obstacle that was put in his path because of the overwhelming love he had for his family.

So when we were on our "Prosperity Walk" and I literally felt like I was going to die, I attempted to tough it out.

When my symptoms subsided I was back in my office that very same night, working even harder.

My body was not going to tell me how things were going to be, I was going to tell it how it was going to be.

That attitude is just part of my being.

As an entrepreneur, one of my primary reasons for having my own business is that I like living life on my own terms and not someone else's.

That is just how I am wired.

This attitude of indifference to MAJOR warning signals my body was sending almost cost me my life, well it did cost me my life as a matter of fact for 1.5 to 2 minutes.

My body was getting ready to show me who the boss really was in a very dramatic way.

I had no idea how quickly the breath can be taken from your body.

Close your eyes.

Now open them.

That's how quickly you can die.

I was about to find that out first hand.

I was about to learn who the Boss really was.

In the next chapter, I talk about the night that changed my life forever. The night of my sudden cardiac arrest, death and revival.

THE NIGHT MY LIFE CHANGED FOREVER

March 20th was the night that my life would be forever changed.

That night, I shut down working in my office a little earlier than normal. It was around 1:00 AM.

One of my nightly rituals is to decompress in our jacuzzi bathtub before going to bed.

When I got into the tub, without any notice, I started to feel like I had indigestion and a hand was slowly moving up my chest to my throat.

I had never felt anything like this before.

I immediately got out of the jacuzzi and headed to bed.

The level of my discomfort only increased, so I went downstairs and got a baby aspirin, came back upstairs and thought I would try the jacuzzi bath one more time.

The discomfort was still holding steady so I got out again and headed back to bed.

I knew by this time something was seriously wrong.

I actually got on my knees to pray and the discomfort really increased.

When I stood up, that is when Vickie woke up from her sleep and asked me what was wrong.

I told her that I was having really bad chest pains and I was going to head downstairs to get a drink of water.

I went downstairs and sat in my office chair for a moment when I felt very nauseous, so I headed to the bathroom.

Walking to the bathroom, I was sweating profusely and I had numbness in my entire left arm which I had never had before.

I know that these were the signs of a heart attack but I was refusing to accept the signs.

Instead, I laid down on the cool tile floor to try and cool down.

That is where I was when Vickie came downstairs.

When I told Vickie that my left arm was completely numb she immediately said, "I am calling 911."

I told her not to do that but to just get a cool wash cloth for my head. But she did not listen. When I heard her on the phone with 911, I got up and went into the bedroom next to the bathroom on our main level and crawled into bed there because I knew at that point the paramedics were coming and there was nothing I could do to stop it.

When the paramedics arrived they hooked me up to an EKG machine and gave me three additional baby aspirins. Based on what my symptoms were they asked me which hospital I wanted to go to. I replied, "I am not going to any hospital" and if I was having a heart attack

What I did not know is that, legally, they are not permitted to give me a diagnosis. But they strongly recommended that I go based on what they were seeing on the EKG and my symptoms, to which I repeated that I was not going to the hospital.

You see, I did not see these gentlemen as men who were trying to save my life. I viewed them as roosters who had come into my home telling me what I was and was not going to do. That does not work with me.

My decision not to go to the hospital only grew more resolute as I gradually began feeling better laying there.

I decided to go to the hospital when they told me that they would probably just do blood work on me to determine whether or not I had actually had a heart attack. That made sense to me and I thought it wouldn't involve much, so I agreed to go – but only if Vickie drove me because I wanted to save the ambulance fee.

At that point Vickie had had enough of my shenanigans and asked me point blank, "Do you want to live or die?"

What I did not realize was that, at that moment, I was already in the process of dying right in front of Vickie's eyes.

I did not know this but my color was getting worse and she had leaned over to the paramedic and said, "He won't make it if I drive him will he?" He shook his head and that is when she put her foot down and asked me if I wanted to live or die.

"Of course I want to live," I told her.

"Well then go to the hospital," she told me firmly.

I want you to know that wives have more power over their husbands than they think.

God has ordained that sacred union for a reason.

Vickie has always backed me up and let me lead but she has a way of speaking to me that lets me know that she means business and had had enough.

This was one of those times.

Wives often see what you can not see, and what my wife saw was that I was literally minutes away from dying and I was not budging.

There is no one that is walking the face of this earth that could have made me get into that ambulance that night except my wife.

If you ask any paramedic when they are called to a home with a husband who has chest pains, the vast majority refuse to go and it is the wife who has to intervene and make their husbands go.

I was no different.

Sensing that Vickie had had enough of my stubbornness I said, "Okay, I will go to the hospital." The paramedics immediately did not give me a chance to reconsider my decision.

They sprung into action.

The paramedic asked me if I could walk the few steps to the stretcher that was located just outside the bedroom door to which I glibly replied, "Not only can I walk to that stretcher but I have a set of weights in my garage and I can bust out a few reps before we leave!"

You have to remember at that moment in time, I was feeling better and thought I had beaten whatever it was that had been bothering me.

"You won't be doing that," was the curt reply of the paramedic who also had had enough of my shenanigans by that time.

When we got to the driveway I noticed that Mark, our neighbor who worked the night shift as a police officer, was home and I knew that Vickie did not know where either one of the two available hospitals were. In her present state I knew it would be better if someone else drove her, so, I made Vickie promise me that she would ask Mark to drive her to the hospital, which she agreed to do.

When we hit the driveway, that weird feeling of indigestion came back and it felt like there were two hands around my neck. It was literally like the death angel was on the top of my chest.

As they loaded me into the back of the ambulance, I blew a kiss to Vickie and thought *'Peas and Carrots forever.'* As they closed the door, I thought this was way too much drama. Little did I know that I was seconds away from going into sudden cardiac arrest and not having a pulse for a minute and a half to 2 minutes. I was seconds away from going to a place from which few people ever return.

CLINICALLY DEAD

I was in the ambulance for no more than a minute when I went into sudden cardiac arrest and had no heart beat or pulse for 1.5 to 2 minutes.

I was clinically dead.

The last words I told the paramedic was, "I feel funny." Next thing I know, I am standing on a train platform between two silver trains.

Two silver trains speeding down the track super fast.

Each train was headed into a tunnel of white light.

On the side of each train was a video of entire my life being shown to me.

It was not being shown in normal speed.

I remember thinking, "This is interesting. Why am I seeing this?"

The next thing I know, I am back in the ambulance looking up into the paramedic's face.

But now, he was sweating like he had been running on a treadmill and there was a controlled chaos going on inside the paramedic van.

He looked down at me and his eyes got as big as saucers and he said "Dude, you're the 1%. Most people never make it back from where you just were."

I remember reasoning, "Well of course I am the 1%, but how did he know? Had he been on my Facebook page?"

I had created an image for my Facebook page that said, "I am the 1%" as my statement against this 99% protest stuff that has been going on, and that was the first thing you saw when you went to my Facebook page.

I had only recently changed it.

I was actually going to make t-shirts that said "I am the 1%".

Please understand that I am not trying to be humorous or glib about the thoughts I was having at that time, but just relating to you what really happened.

You tell me what the odds are that I had created and installed an image on my Facebook page that says " I am the 1%" then, soon, I am clinically dead for 1.5 to 2 minutes and the first thing that the paramedic says to me when I am revived was that I am the 1%!

Folks, there are no such things as "coincidences" and we do frame our world with the words that we speak over our life!

Turns out that only 1% of all out-of-hospital sudden cardiac arrests actually survive.

The paramedic then shared with me that they had lost me for about 1.5 to 2 minutes, and had told me to hold on, and that they had to defibrillate me two times to get me back.

Most people do not make it back after 1 minute let alone almost 2 minutes, but I did, and I did so without spot or blemish.

The paramedics were very surprised that I was able to talk and remember where I was, but you see this is what they did not know at the time ...

When I was loaded in the back of the ambulance and the doors closed, the ambulance did not leave right away. Vickie knew something was wrong.

All she could do was pace on the side of that ambulance and call on the name of Jesus.

"Jesus, Jesus, Jesus," was all she could say.

She had no idea what was going on in the back of that ambulance but she knew something was wrong and she knew who to call on. Jesus.

All of a sudden, the Fire Department truck that had left before us, came roaring back down the street and a firefighter jumped out of the truck and ran to the back of the ambulance and jumped in. Vickie then knew for certain that something was wrong. She tells the lady firefighter that was standing outside the ambulance, "I know something is wrong, please tell me what is going on, that's my husband in there and I need to know!"

"Ma'am, your husband died but they were able to bring him back and the paramedic needed help working on him. That is why we came back so fast."

At this same time – some 1,300 miles away in Detroit Michigan – my sister, Renee, was out of town on a business trip when the Lord woke her up to pray. She had no idea who she was praying for, only that she was to pray...which she did.

What those two paramedics did not know, what they could not know, is that a third man had entered that ambulance. But this was not just any man.

This man had conquered hell, death and the grave and held all power and authority.

When that sandaled foot from Galilee entered the ambulance, everything changed!

I assure you that there is no more hopeless situation than to be clinically dead for 1.5 to 2 minutes with no pulse and or heartbeat. But, Praise God that it ain't over till it's REALLY over and that God has the final say!

Your situation may be hopeless. You may be at the end of your rope. You may think that things can never change or that it is too late for you...and you would be wrong!

Maybe it is a business or a marriage or a dream that you think is dead, but it is never too late for God to intervene.

Maybe you have had a negative health report or your family is in chaos.

As long as you have breath in your body, or in my case no breath in my body, when God shows up...things change!

Change can happen in a moment...in the twinkling of an eye.

Vickie, my wife, loves the Lord and He often wakes her in the early morning hours to pray, as he did my sister.

And she gets up and prays.

It does not matter if it is cold out and the bed is warm or that she is too tired. She will get up without question and go into her prayer room and pray.

Now, the Lord does not do that with me or most guys that I know.

Because if he did, the conversation would go something like this: "Lord, you want me to get out of this warm and comfy bed to pray and you're not going to tell me who I am praying for or why I am praying? Come on Lord, is this really you?"

But women, especially praying women, do not respond the same way.

They do not hesitate to jump out of that bed the moment they hear him whisper, "Daughter, I need you to pray."

There are husbands, sons and daughters that are alive that are walking the streets right now because of a praying mother, grandmother, sister or wife.

I am one of them.

The Lord really wants those praying women to know that their prayers are not in vain, and that there is a reason each and every time He calls you to pray.

Even though others may not understand it or even criticize you for getting up to pray at odd times of the night, you can trust that He has a reason and He hears your prayers.

As I said before, I was without a pulse or heartbeat for 1.5 to 2 minutes and had to be shocked. I had to have chest compressions to get my heart re-started, and when I came back into that ambulance, it was controlled chaos.

We were en route to the hospital and they were telling me to "hold on."

I clearly remember that I had no fear at all...

I had no fear and I had no plans on going anywhere either.

I know that I had to stay calm, and to be quite honest, I was disgusted with myself for dying the first time, so I did not want to do it again.

I remember shaking my head from side to side in disgust thinking I cannot believe this just happened to me.

I was in the Army. They train you to stay calm in all situations but I can tell you that I had a peace that passes all understanding that only the Lord can give.

It was like being in a boat with an intense storm raging outside, but inside the boat I had calm and peace.

I have had a chance to tell others that, had I come back into that ambulance without knowing the Lord, then that would have been the most frightening experience I could ever have had.

I really would not wish that experience on anyone.

The sirens were going, the radio was crackling with the paramedics giving my vital signs and estimated time of arrival to the hospital and whoever was driving was doing so with an extreme sense of urgency.

To be told in that environment that you had just died and had to be shocked two times and that you are one of the lucky ones to make it back would cause anyone to be naturally fearful.

But for me, Isaiah 43.2 literally came to life for me in that ambulance.

Isaiah 43:2
"When you pass through the waters, I will be with you; and through the rivers, they will not overflow you. When you walk through the fire, you will not be scorched, nor will the flame burn you."

That is not the time to be making deals with the Lord and I made no deals with the Lord during my time in that ambulance.

I had no idea when they loaded me into the back of that ambulance the first time that I would go into sudden cardiac arrest and literally not have a pulse or heartbeat for 1.5 to 2 minutes and be seconds away from eternity.

People act like they have all the time in the world to get right with God. Well, I am here to tell you that you don't.

If you're reading this and you know in your heart that you are not right with God then please understand this: there are no coincidences with God.

You are reading this for a reason.

It is better to have Him and not need Him than to need Him and not have Him.

Because of my sudden cardiac arrest, the decision was made to take me to HealthPark Hospital which actually specializes in treating the heart.

So let's talk about what happened there in the next chapter.

CARDIAC SEAL TEAM

After what seemed like forever but in reality was a very quick drive, the ambulance arrived at the emergency room entrance of HealthPark Medical Center.

HealthPark is a designated Chest Pain Center specializing in all areas of heart care. As a major trauma center they have a team of cardiac specialists on-call at all times who are able to respond to the trauma center within minutes of an emergency notification – ready to administer treatment within a victim's very narrow window of time. I refer to them as a "Cardiac Seal Team". They were ready and waiting for me to arrive.

Within five minutes of my arrival, the cardiologist who was on call arrived and assured me that I was in good hands and that as soon as the two other team members arrived we would be going into surgery immediately (before I could change my mind, I surmised).

The first thing that I noticed was the posture of everyone on that team.

They let me know that I was in the right place and that they were going to take good care of me.

They meant it and I knew it.

I cannot begin to express to you the unexpected level of calmness that their posture, the confidence they displayed, allowed me. It was highly reassuring for me at that moment in time.

It was striking. I sensed that this was their playground and they were the best at what they did.

I knew I was in the right place at the right time.

On the other hand, I felt somewhat guilty as it had to be at least 3:00 AM by then, and I absolutely do not like people to be inconvenienced because of me.

This Cardiac Seal team had been called in because of me. They had been at their homes probably sleeping. Because of me, they had to get up and get to the hospital, so I kept thanking everyone and apologizing that they had to be called in just because of me.

I attempted to lighten the mood with humor and get folks laughing but, above all else, I wanted them to understand that I was thankful and to let them know that I appreciated them.

I asked if my wife had arrived yet and they said that she had just gotten there. I asked if they could please get her and they said yes.

At my bedside, I asked Vickie if they told her what had happened to me. She said that they had. I apologized to her for this happening and for causing her to go through this dreadful experience.

I also asked to speak to Mark, our neighbor the police officer, who willingly got out of bed to drive Vickie to the hospital. I thanked him for doing that and apologized that he, too, had been inconvenienced by me.

It felt like I had only been there for ten minutes before the two other team members arrived and I was being wheeled off to surgery.

They responded to me with an extreme sense of urgency, as if there was no time to lose.

As they were wheeling me to surgery, I saw team members speaking to Vickie and I asked if it would be okay to stop a moment for Vickie and I to pray together.

As a man, I am used to being strong for my wife and family, to being the leader and not showing any weakness. Yet, here I was facing the harsh reality that I might not be those things again, that this may very well be the last time I even see my wife.

At that moment in time, I faced the harsh reality that I may very well not make it through this surgery, and if that was the case…

I wanted my last moment with Vickie to be one of us praying... together.

Peas and Carrots Forever.

That sweet moment that Vickie and I shared in prayer as a husband and wife is a memory that I will cherish forever.

Vickie cried as she prayed for me, and how she got through that prayer I do not know.

It was one of the most poignant moments of our entire marriage.

There are times in your life that are what I call "defining moments".

A moment when you are at the crossroads of your destiny.

At that precise moment in time I was standing directly at my crossroad to eternity, and we both knew it.

Even as I type this, I get very emotional thinking of that overwhelming moment.

There is no force in the universe compared to that of a husband and wife who come together and pray.

None.

It was the ultimate expression of love not only for each other but also for the Lord.

After we prayed and repeated our "I love yous" they wheeled me through the entrance to the surgery room which they call a Cath Lab.

I was told that they were going to perform an angioplasty on me. I would be awake as they ran a line up through my femoral artery in the thigh area to my heart to view what the issue was and repair it. If they could not fix what was wrong then the next option would be open heart surgery.

Again, the professionalism of this Cardiac Seal team lead by the cardiologist was fully on display as they proceeded with haste.

With an angioplasty you are awake during the entire procedure.

There is a numbing agent applied to the thigh where the incision will be and, because the artery has no nerves in it, there is no pain during the surgery.

But there is fear...oh yes there is.

Up until then I had no fear, but the moment I was faced with my own personal mortality, things changed dramatically.

In the operating room, I kept my eyes open for the entire surgery, which took over two hours. I did not want to close my eyes because I was afraid that, if I did, when I opened them I might find myself floating above the hospital bed which meant that I died...again.

They told me that some people actually fall asleep during their surgery, but I determined that it was not going to happen during mine.

I had already died one time that night. I did not want to die a second time.

So I laid there the entire time with my eyes open, and praying.

I prayed throughout the time I was in surgery.

After the surgery was completed they told me that I had a 100% blockage in my left ascending artery.

That blockage is commonly referred to as the Widow Maker because it is fatal the majority of times.

So, yet another miracle, that I had survived such a severe blockage.

They told me that they had to insert two stents in that artery and leave a pump in to ease the strain on my heart as I recovered.

ME AND THE LORD IN THE INTENSIVE CARE UNIT

As they wheeled me into the recovery room, I thought I saw the room number that was between the sliding glass doors. So I informed the nurses that I operated on the quantum level and could tell them the room number I was just put in.

They laughed and said, "Ok, what room number are we in?"

I gave them the number that I thought I had seen but, surprisingly, they laughed and replied, "You're not even close!"

So much for my quantum level accuracy. But I was alive and I was thankful.

Nevertheless, I knew my journey was far from over as I was wheeled into the ICU.

After they wheeled me into the ICU the idea of being there was utterly surreal to me. I have been in several ICU's as a visitor, but never as a patient.

I was being wheeled into my new reality.

This was something I was going to have to face whether I liked it or not.

It took the staff about 45 minutes to get me hooked up to all of the machines and to ensure that I was stabilized before they would allow Vickie to come in for our first visit.

Far from being out of the woods the possibility existed that, if I took a turn for the worse, I would have to be rushed back into surgery.

My back hurt. It was in a lot of pain from laying flat and not being able to move during the two hours in surgery. And, because the sciatic nerve is next to the femoral artery where the angioplasty was done, my right thigh felt like it was on fire.

My ejection fraction percentage was only 30%.

"Ejection fraction"(EF) is the fraction of blood pumped out of a ventricle with each heartbeat.

To put that into perspective, the average adult male has an EF of 50% to 60%. So my heart was pumping half the blood that it should have.

The balloon pump inserted into my chest was taking much of the workload and stress off of my heart.

I was shocked at the shallowness of my breathing, however.

In addition, I was instructed to keep my right leg as straight and immobile as possible to prevent any potential for a life-threatening bleed. This was the critical area where the angioplasty had been done as well as insertion point of the balloon pump that was going to help my heart do some of the pumping to relieve my heart of some unnecessary stress.

There was a long road ahead of me in ICU and I knew it.

When they finally allowed Vickie in to see me I was absolutely thrilled.

"Peas and Carrots" together again and I immediately shifted into husband mode. I was concerned about her and wanted her to go home and get some rest.

Of course, Vickie had no intention of going anywhere. I cautioned her that this was going to be a long journey and it was going to be important that she take care of herself.

If it were up to Vickie she would never have left the hospital at all. Thankfully, she listened to what I had to say about the stressful road ahead of us. I was telling her what we would be facing for the foreseeable future.

Hospitals are very draining, especially on family members. But the fact is that the real journey begins when you leave the hospital, not when you are in it.

I did not want Vickie drained and physically ill when I came home and would need her the most.

So Vickie agreed to go home and get some rest, but not until the doctors made their morning rounds that day.

Another thing that I asked Vickie to do for me was to go online to my Facebook page and update my status with the news that I had had a heart attack and to please pray.

By posting that one message, my family and friends knew instantly what had happened and they started praying.

I have friends that I went to school with over 30 years ago who prayed and left encouraging messages to Vickie and me of their love and support.

There was one message that touched me to the core, and that was from a girl I went to high school with. Sue Wasielewski. She has been engaged in a brutal battle with cancer for a long time.

Sue let me know she was praying for me.

In the midst of Sue's battle she did not focus exclusively on her own situation, she took the time to say a heartfelt prayer on my behalf and it meant everything to me.

I was to stay in the Intensive Care Unit for the next five days and, instead of going into graphic detail, I would rather share with you the important things that occurred while I was recovering in the ICU.

That first night in the ICU was a particular challenge because I did not trust myself to close my eyes.

When I did close them I would awaken with what felt like electric shocks.

Literally, I would feel a short burst of electricity going through my body.

The best way for me to describe it is like when you have just fallen asleep and something wakes you up suddenly. That jolt-like feeling is what I felt when I would close my eyes.

My theory on this was that it was a residual feeling from the two electric shocks the paramedic crew had to administer to revive me.

Also, my chest and ribs were extremely sore from the chest compressions (CPR) that had to be used to revive me in the ambulance.

Mentally, there was one bridge I wasn't crossing. I was not accepting the fact that I had, indeed, died and that I had to be brought back.

I just flat out refused to accept the death experience in my mind.

That was until after Vickie visited the fire station to get the names of the men who had so heroically saved my life some days earlier.

Vickie told me on the phone, "Yes, Sweetheart. I just spoke to the paramedic who saved your life and, yes, you did die. You did not have a pulse or heartbeat for 1.5 to 2 minutes, and he had to shock you two times and do chest compressions to bring you back."

That was too much for me.

I could no longer deny what had happened.

I began weeping uncontrollably and feebly told Vickie that I had to go.

My reaction at that point was so intense that Vickie was concerned I might be having another heart attack. I managed to squeeze out a subdued, "No, I'm just too overwhelmed with emotion. I need to go."

Unworthy, humble and small, I just wept. I began thanking my Lord and Savior for not only sparing my life but for returning to me His gifts of unimpaired speech, of a right mind and physical strength, as well as for protecting me from being paralyzed.

> **In that one moment I knew what the Lord had done for me and it was overwhelming.**

It was in that moment that I asked the Lord to give Sue, my high school friend who has been battling cancer, the same miracle of life that He had given me.

That moment is etched in my mind forever. I will never forget it.

Not ever.

It was me and the Lord in that ICU room and He had my full attention.

I knew He had saved me for a reason.

I never asked one time, "Why did this happen to me?"

I am only 48 years old.

I do not drink or smoke.

Not one time did I ask the "why me?" question or view myself as a victim.

My only question was, "How can this be used to HIS Glory and Purpose?"

Because I knew I had been saved for a reason.

I knew one of the initial things I was being called to do was to write this book and, from that moment, the Lord began to pour out and reveal to me the things I was to share in this book.

The refrain, "It ain't over till it's REALLY over!" rung in my mind.

He impressed that He really wants His people, the ones called by His name, to be reminded of an important and powerful fact ☐ and they need to remind each other of this: Regardless how your situation looks to you (or others) in the moment, always know that...

"It ain't over till it's REALLY over!

"As long as there is breath in your body, and even when there is not breath in your body, there is still HOPE!"

Being clinically dead without a heartbeat or pulse for 1.5 to 2 minutes is about as bleak and dire as it gets, yet it was not too late for Jesus to intervene and give me a miracle!

People are in need of Him more than ever. Yet we have become desensitized to the real, supernatural power of Jesus Christ to step into any situation and change it.

Change can happen in a moment, in a twinkling of an eye, but not if you do not believe it can or if you give up.

I have already shared with you the fact that, if it were not for my Vickie, I would not have even gotten into that ambulance in the first place, and I would have died. If Vickie wasn't home, I wouldn't have made it because I would have never gotten into that ambulance unless she was there.

The Lord also wants folks, especially the young kids, to know how much importance He puts on the sanctity of marriage. What they see happening in Hollywood with people marrying for three months and then getting divorced is not His plan.

Vickie and I agreeing in prayer before my surgery is what it's all about.

There is nothing more powerful in this world than a husband and wife who are joined as ONE who come together in their moment of crisis and pray!

Everything you have read in this book was revealed to me while I was in the ICU.

Everything.

From calling on His name when you are in a time of trouble (Vickie pacing beside the ambulance while I was without a pulse or heartbeat).

The praying woman that He awakens at all hours of the night to pray for something or somebody without even knowing the reason why (my sister's prayers at 2:00 AM for an unknown purpose).

The fact that there are no such things as coincidences (if I go into cardiac arrest anywhere but in that ambulance, I do not make it).

This entire book was revealed to me in that Intensive Care Unit. It was not intended to be a book about a heart attack or a guy who survived sudden cardiac arrest or a Widow Maker, and I knew it.

Less than 1% of all people who experience an out of hospital sudden cardiac arrest survive and less than 10% survive the widow maker.

And I had survived both against overwhelming odds without spot or blemish and I knew God had a reason for sparing my life.

As part of my business I had already written a best-selling program, spoken professionally, done countless radio interviews, created videos, designed and built direct response websites for people in business, and was already an expert in internet marketing.

So I knew one of the reasons that I was left with my talents intact was to get this message out.

The only thing I did not have while in the ICU room was the title of the book, but I trusted that it would come later.

The other thing I knew I had to do was to make sure the paramedic crew that saved my life was properly acknowledged.

It was important that they be honored as heroes.

After a couple of days in ICU, Ray, the paramedic who had saved my life, popped his head into my room to check on me. He had just completed transporting someone else there…and all I could say at the time was "thank you", which did not seem quite adequate to me. It was important that the world know that Ray was a hero and I was committed to seeing him acknowledged as such.

I spent a total of five days in the ICU room and during that time I did my best to bring laughter and joy to everyone I met there and to let them know how much I appreciated them.

I would tell the nurses who came to stick me and draw blood that I would be a gentleman and not scream until after they left the room. Each time they left, I would wait a few moments and let out a fake scream.

I was cared for by some of the best nurses on the planet and, when I left the ICU, I knew in my heart what I was supposed to do.

TIME TO GO HOME

In all, I was in the ICU room for five days and a regular hospital room for two days. Everyone was quite taken with the story of what had happened to me.

They loved hearing my story and I loved sharing it with them.

I saw firsthand how my miraculous story impacted people.

I was visited by the sweetest, compassionate lady chaplain.

She had looked into my room and asked if I wanted a Catholic blessing because someone had called her office and requested that a Catholic blessing be given to the person in my room number.

I told her with a warm smile, "Well, I am not Catholic and while I do not mind a blessing, I do not want to take someone else's blessing if by chance you got the room number wrong."

She asked if I minded if she came in and talked and I said, "No problem."

She listened to my story of what had happened to me with such compassion in her eyes and told me what a beautiful and powerful story it was. She asked if I minded if she prayed for me. In that hospital room we had the sweetest moment of prayer.

It did not matter to her that I was not a Catholic. What mattered to her was that we both loved the Lord, and we both knew a miracle had happened in my life.

After a week, it was time for me to be discharged from the hospital.

I was more than ready to get home and 'take the hill again"...until Vickie pulled the car up to the curb and I had to stand up and leave the wheelchair that had been used to bring me down.

It was then as I stood up that I realized I was now leaving the safety net or "life line" of the hospital.

It was easier being brave in the hospital.

While I was in the hospital, if anything happened to me, I knew that everything would be okay because my support system was right there.

Now, as I entered the car, I knew I would not have that safety net anymore.

I was very aware of that fact but it really did not impact me fully until the moment I stood up and relinquished that wheelchair.

Vickie and I decided to stop by the pharmacy to get all of my medicines on the way home. I really did not want to have to go back out again once we got home and Vickie sure did not want to leave me once we got home.

At the pharmacy I got out of the car and went in, too, and soon started to feel unwell. I saw that they had a blood pressure machine. I figured I would check mine out and was stunned to see that is was 90 over 60.

Way too low.

I felt like I was going to pass out, so I remained seated until Vickie was done and we went home.

We have a female dog named Lexus, who adores her mommy and daddy and is super loyal to us.

Whenever Vickie and I have been away on a trip, we have had a neighbor watch Lexus and I have paid a price whenever I have picked her up.

She gets overly excited and starts nipping me. This is her way of letting me know that, even though she loves being at our neighbor's house, she did not appreciate being left behind.

Vickie was concerned about how Lexus would react to seeing me again and, with me being on blood thinners, we could not have her nipping me.

I told Vickie that I would stay in the back seat of the car and that she could just let Lexus out and I would call to her from the back seat.

Vickie was not sure that that was the smartest thing to do but I was pretty sure that things would be fine.

So, when we arrived home Vickie let Lexus out, I called to her, and she got into the back seat with me very gently and simply gave me a kiss.

Dogs know.

While it was good to be home, it was important that Vickie and I have an understanding moving forward.

I understood that she was going to have me on "lockdown" and I got that.

But I wanted her to know that I would be 100% honest with her regarding my physical condition and how I felt.

I felt it was important that she knew that I would not sugar coat anything about how I was feeling at any time.

Vickie was naturally on edge because she had been through so much emotional trauma dealing with everything that had just happened to me.

I think that it was important to let her know that at all times, when it came to how I was feeling, I would tell her honestly what was going on with me.

She and everyone else already knew about the discomfort I was feeling in my chest area, which was attributed to the chest compressions that were done on me by the paramedic crew.

However, that low blood pressure issue was plaguing me in the afternoons that followed.

I would wake up in the morning feeling fine and take all of my medications, and then in the afternoon my blood pressure would drop way too low.

Fortunately, Vickie's good friend who used to be a nurse visited at our request and confirmed that my blood pressure was too low. She told us to call the doctor and let them know because she felt it had to be the medications that were causing my low blood pressure.

We did, and the doctor had me stop a couple of the meds and I no longer had the issue with the low blood pressure.

My main goal when I got home was to NOT have a relapse, nor to fall into any type of post-heart attack depression.

Vickie was told at the hospital that there was a very good chance I would suffer from some sort of depression, like a post traumatic stress condition. This is a common occurrence among people who have gone through what I did.

Well, that's all I needed to know – that depression is common – to make me committed NOT to go through it!

Remember, my DNA dictates that, if the herd is all going one way, it is a sure thing I will be leading the charge the other way.

So, those were my two primary goals when I got home and, of course, to write this book and to see to it that the paramedic crew that saved my life was honored as the heroes they are.

Walking was very important in my rehab. Vickie and I (and Lexus) made sure that I walked to the end of the block and back in the morning.

I knew that I had to take the block before I could take the hill.

The task of writing this book was always on my mind but I still did not have the title. I trusted that the Lord would give it to me at the right time.

A day or two after I got home we took a drive to the local grocery store and I ran into Steve from the pool supply store. He looked like he was looking at a ghost when he saw me. He already knew what had happened to me but, when I shared the details with him, tears welled up in his eyes because he was so moved. I gave him a big hug there in the store.

As I walked to the car, the Lord spoke to my heart and said, "That's why this story must be told."

I knew.

I had the story. I even had the tag line, "It ain't over till it's REALLY over". But I didn't have a title.

Nothing was coming to me at all.

That was until I got a phone call from my good friend, Stephen, who lives in Australia.

After catching up with me and sharing the details of my story with him, Stephen declared out of nowhere, "I have the title of your book, Mate."

You could have knocked me over with a stick at that moment because I had not mentioned to Stephen that I was searching for a title to the book! He just blurted it out!

"God Says When".

I knew it the second I heard it that this was the title of the book!

I also knew it would be much more than a title of a book.

I literally saw in my spirit those people who have been told that their situation is hopeless wearing shirts with the words "God Says When" or a wrist bands inscribed with "God Says When" into their hospital rooms.

Listen, I understand that you might be uncomfortable telling your doctor that you don't accept his/her diagnosis that there is no hope for you.

I get that.

But everyone can wear a shirt or wrist band with three simple words on it.

"God Says When!"

Three simple but powerful words that let anyone who sees them know where you stand. Especially when it comes to anyone who needs a miracle, or if your situation is perceived as hopeless.

I am not just talking about folks with health issues either.

"God Says When" will forever be associated with folks who were faced with impossible, even overwhelming, odds only to see the Lord intervene miraculously on their behalf.

Maybe God gave you a dream that you think has died, or you think that things are never going to change, or that there's no use in even trying.

Your breakthrough is closer than you think.

Don't ever give up on God because He will never give up on you.

His timing is impeccable and, just when you think all hope is lost, He can step in and change any situation in a moment, just like He did for me.

Incidentally, I believe that my story won't be the last "God Says When" story.

I trust that my next book will be a collection of "God Says When" stories from people around the world.

It is no coincidence that you are reading these words at this time.

Never give up. It is never too late for YOUR miracle!

GREATEST HONOR OF MY LIFE

On May 24, which happened to be Vickie's and my 21st wedding anniversary, I was honored to be able to present the Phoenix Award to the paramedic, Ray Wiegand, who saved my life.

Lee County gives what they call the Phoenix Award to any paramedic who has a medical save in the line of duty. This particular ceremony was extra special because it coincided with EMS week, the week set aside all across the country to appreciate and honor all EMS personnel.

Vickie and I were invited to this event and we were both were very emotional just thinking about it. Quite honestly, I did not know how I was going to get through it without breaking down and crying.

I mean what do you say to the man that did not give up on you?

It is common knowledge that most people who are clinically dead for over a minute do not come back, but Ray refused to be denied.

It is amazing that Ray was able to do everything he did to me during that 1.5 to 2 minutes that I was clinically dead.

Thank God for Ray's persistence. He never gave up on me.

So you can understand why just the idea of attending this special event would cause both Vickie and I to become teary-eyed.

But my sense of teetering on an emotional fence was quickly changed to one of pure exhilaration when I was asked to present the award to Ray myself.

Being no stranger to public speaking, I agreed to do so without hesitation. From that instant I was in a completely different mode because I wanted to do a great job for Ray and I could not do that if I was overly emotional.

I was thrilled that Ray's family was there along with his peers and I wanted them all to know, from someone on the receiving side, what a hero Ray was.

So when it came time to present the award I was called up in front and I asked Vickie to accompany me. I asked Vickie to speak first.

Vickie was very emotional but did a fantastic job and then it was my turn to speak.

I shared the story of what had happened to me and concluded by sharing that, when I was growing up, my heroes were never movie stars, sports stars or rock stars, but my family.

My mom

My dad.

I then added that the paramedic crew who saved my life would forever be part of that list – and that Ray would be at the very top.

I wrapped it up by expressing that, at the end of a man or woman's life, you will be faced with three simple questions:

Did I live...Did I really live?

Did I love...Did I really love?

And did I matter? Did my life matter and have meaning?

You are responsible for the first two but, on the last one, if you are an EMS paramedic it is a certainty that your life matters and does have meaning!

I then was able to present Ray with his Phoenix Award medal, which was one of the absolute greatest honors of my life.

I am very clear that the Lord spared my life that morning but He used Ray as His instrument.

THE REST OF THE STORY

You can actually see the local news report video of that event on our website, GodSaysWhen.com.

That morning God gave me three miracles. First, I was the 1% who actually survive a sudden cardiac arrest outside a hospital. Then after being clinically dead for 1.5 to 2 minutes, I was brought back without spot or blemish with no paralysis, brain or memory loss. Finally, I was one of the 10% who survive the widow maker blockage of the left ascending artery.

The odds were against me but God was for me and so was my wife.

My wife truly saved my life that morning because if she was not there I would not have made it.

My side of the story is complete, but there is someone else you really need to hear from and that is my beautiful wife of 21 years, Vickie Bradley.

Vickie is a powerful woman of God who actually started a woman's prayer group in Chicago on Saturday mornings at the church we were a part of, the Leadership Lighthouse Church of All Nations.

In the beginning sometimes Vickie would be the only woman to show up. Yet she was faithful and her ladies prayer group grew to be very powerful and anointed.

One thing I learned is that things happen when women pray.

Vickie Bradley loves the Lord and she knows how to pray.

Vickie is one of those ladies the Lord likes to wake up at odd hours of the night to pray without knowing why or for whom they are praying. She does so without hesitation.

I tell people I had the easy part in this "God Says When" situation. I cannot even imagine what it felt like for Vickie to be told that I had died but was able to be brought back. I can't imagine the emotional trauma she endured.

So I asked Vickie to share with you her side of the story, one that only she could tell.

Enjoy!

BELIEVE ME, YOU ARE NEVER ALONE

When I woke early the morning of March 20, 2012, I didn't realize that my life would never be the same.

My husband, TC, came to bed at 1:00 AM. I know it was God that stirred me awake. I looked at my husband and asked him if he was all right.

He said no, that he was having chest pains. I said, "Let's go to the hospital."

He said no, that he was going to get a glass of water.

Sitting up on the side of the bed, I shook my head and exclaimed, "What!" out loud to myself. "What just happened?"

I got out of bed and, while I was walking toward the bedroom door to go downstairs to check on him, he called my name.

I said, "Oh Jesus, help me." and tried to go faster, but it was like my body didn't want to go faster.

Downstairs, I found TC sitting with his head over the bathroom toilet.

His color didn't look good to me and I asked him if he was still having chest pain.

He said yes and that he needed a cold wash cloth.

I put one on his head after I wiped off his face and neck.

I asked him if he had any feeling in his arms. He said no. I told him I was calling 911, to which he said no again.

I said, "Oh Jesus, help me." My heart was beating so fast but, knowing that God was with me, I took a deep breath and said to myself, "Vickie, get it together."

My mind and heart were going 100 miles an hour, so many things were racing through my mind. I kept shaking my head. I couldn't believe this was happening. I was in shock!

Then I called 911 and told the dispatcher that my husband was having chest pains and no feeling in his arms and that his color didn't look good.

The dispatcher asked me where he was and if he was conscious. I told her yes.

I told her he was in the bathroom. She asked me if he was talking. I again told her yes.

She assured me that help was on the way but that I needed to turn our lights on outside, have the doors open and if I had any pets to put them up.

I went back to bathroom and TC was not there.

I called for him and he had gone to the bed in the downstairs bedroom.

"What are you doing?" I asked him. "Why did you move from the bathroom into the bedroom?"

He said he wasn't going to have them see him in the bathroom.

He said he was feeling better, but I told him not to move.

As I took my nightgown off and threw on some clothes I kept shouting out to my husband, "Are you ok?" He kept saying yes.

I kept running back and forth from the door to the bedroom, all the time asking my husband, "Are you all right?"

I kept thinking that the ambulance should be here by now. I kept praying and calling on the name of Jesus!

I knew God was with me, my spirit was at peace but my heart was screaming out, which was my flesh. I was really scared because I was letting my flesh take over.

I know it was only minutes since I called the 911, but it seemed like forever.

The paramedics and fire rescue teams arrived and came into the house with a stretcher.

I said, "Thank God."

From the front door to the bedroom, I kept saying, "Oh Jesus, help us." I could feel that He was there but my heart and mind were screaming because, once again, I let my flesh take over.

My body started to tremble and my voice was shaking. One of the paramedics cautioned, "You need to take a deep breath and calm down."

I told him okay, I knew that and I thanked him.

I just stood there for a second to get myself together. I knew I had to stay strong for my husband. His life depended on it.

They took my husband's vitals, hooked him up to the heart monitor and asked him what seemed like a lot of questions.

They asked him what hospital he wanted to go to, HealthPark or Gulf Coast, which they said were the best for heart issues.

TC told them firmly, "I am not going to the hospital."

Then he asked the paramedics, "What does that machine say? Am I having a heart attack?"

The paramedic said, "I am not a doctor but I highly recommend you go the hospital now."

After they explained to him that they would probably do blood work on him to determine if he had had a heart attack, he agreed to go but only if I drove him and that we would be going to the Cape Coral hospital since it was closer.

The paramedic said "Sir, if you go to Cape Coral Hospital there is a great possibility they will have to transfer you to HealthPark or Gulf Coast hospital anyway because they are equipped for heart trauma patients."

I wanted to let my husband know that this was serious and that we were wasting precious time because he was being so stubborn.

I looked at the paramedic and asked, "In your honest opinion he would not make it if I drove him, would he?"

He shook his head no.

I said, "Thank you so much for being honest with me."

At this point, my husband's refusal to go to the hospital was really troubling me. To make matters worse, his color was not looking good again. I knew he was dying right before my very eyes, so I looked into his face and asked, "Do you want to live or die?"

He said, "Of course, I want to live."

I said, "Okay, then stop this and let's go to the hospital right now!"

He said, "Okay. I will go."

The paramedics sprung into action as if they wanted to get him on the stretcher before he changed his mind.

They asked him if he could walk over to the stretcher since it would not fit through the bedroom door.

My husband told them he could walk to the garage and "hang and bang" with some weights that he had out there.

They all exclaimed, "Oh no you don't. We can't have that!"

I looked at the paramedics and said, "Take him to whichever hospital you think would be the best for my husband."

As they were rolling my husband out, the paramedics asked me if I was okay to drive and I told them I was fine. I am stubborn, too, and don't want anyone to go out of their way for me.

As they wheeled him out of the house I told my husband that I loved him and, with tears in my eyes, I blew him a kiss.

They then they closed the door of the ambulance.

I ran in to let our dog, Lexus, out of the other bedroom and I kept praying and calling on The Name of Jesus.

I then felt such a peace and know that Jesus was holding me through all of this.

Then I noticed that the ambulance hadn't pulled out of our driveway yet, and I thought to myself, "Why aren't they leaving?"

I knew that, even though they had to hook him up to everything before they left, it seemed to me that this was taking far too much time.

"Why is the ambulance not moving?"

I started to pace back and forth in the driveway praying and calling on the name of Jesus because the ambulance was not moving and I did not know why.

Then I saw the Fire Rescue truck come flying back down the street. The driver got out and ran to the back of the ambulance, jumped in and closed the door behind him.

The lady firefighter came over to me and I asked her what was going on because I knew something was not right.

She told me that my husband had died but that they had just managed to bring him back alive!

She proceeded to caution me, "I really don't think you should be driving." I knew she was right because I was shaking all over.

Once again my mind and heart racing incredibly fast.

Then the paramedic came out of the back of the ambulance and said, "We are going to have to go to Cape Coral Hospital," not realizing that I was standing there.

He was telling the Fire Department Rescue where they needed to go.

Knowing that this wasn't the best option from our conversation earlier in the house, I said, "Oh no, please don't take him to Cape Coral Hospital."

My mind was asking, "Okay, Vickie, what are you going to do if TC doesn't make it?"

I couldn't even go there! My heart was breaking into a millions pieces.

I said to myself, "Get your act together. You have to keep it together to get through this ... with God's help."

Then I went into the street to see which neighbor's lights were still on, to ask someone drive me to the hospital.

The lights were on at the house right next door.

The fire rescue lady said she would accompany me next door, for which I thanked her.

I rang the doorbell and knocked on the door. I really was hoping that I wasn't waking them up.

Jeanette came to the door and I apologized to her for disturbing her at this hour but explained that TC was on his way to the hospital. I said that I thought TC had had a heart attack, that I was told he died in the ambulance and that they had just resuscitated him.

I told her that I knew I couldn't drive now and asked if someone could take me to Cape Coral Hospital.

She yelled for her son, Mark (a Cape Coral Police Officer), and told him that TC had a heart attack and we needed him to drive me to the hospital.

I thanked her so much for all of this and she said not to worry about Lexus (our dog). She would take care of her.

I thanked the lady firefighter so much for helping me through all of this, and for being honest with me about everything.

I told Jeanette that I would put Lexus back into the house while Mark got ready to take me and thanked her once again.

I gave Lexus kisses and hugs, told her I would be back and I kept nervously stroking her fur, knowing she knew something was wrong.

I know dogs are very smart and are great pets to have.

Mark came out and I asked him if he wanted to drive my car. He said he would drive his truck.

I apologized to Mark for waking them up at this early hour but I couldn't drive to the hospital. He reassured me not worry about that.

Heading toward Cape Coral Hospital, we saw the Fire Rescue Pick-up truck coming down one of the main roads toward us. We didn't know why.

They were coming back to let us know that the doctors at HealthPark had directed them to take us there since TC had been stabilized.

I remember that I kept talking to Mark on the way to the hospital, knowing I was not making any sense at all. I kept repeating, "My husband has got to make it!"

When we arrived at the hospital, Mark dropped me off at the emergency entrance while he parked his truck.

I ran in and went up to an attendant and told him who I was. He said TC wasn't there in the hospital but could still be in the ambulance outside. My heart sank, and I thought it had just stopped. It was breaking.

The man in the emergency room asked me to sit down and I told him I couldn't.

Mark came in and I told him that TC wasn't there but may still be outside.

Mark looked at me and said, "Vickie, do not follow me. Stay here while I check."

I said, "Oh Jesus, please do not let TC be dead. Let him live and not die."

I was really losing it thinking, "What am I am going to do now if he is dead?"

Mark came back in and told me there wasn't an ambulance outside. I said, "Thank You, Jesus."

I asked the man in the emergency room if my husband was possibly at HealthPark. He said that yes, he was at HealthPark Medical Center.

Mark headed to HealthPark Medical Center and, on the way, I had to start thinking about what I was going to do if TC didn't make it through this.

Mark let me off at the emergency entrance of HealthPark. I told the girl at the front desk who I was and she escorted me right to my husband.

At that time, I didn't see the paramedics who were sitting behind the nurse's station.

This was the first time I saw my husband since he was rolled into the ambulance.

He was laughing and joking with everyone.

I didn't know if I wanted to hit, hug or kiss him after seeing him laughing and joking around.

He looked at me and asked me if I knew what had happened.

I told him that I knew.

The ER doctor told me that they had him stabilized and assured me that TC was in good hands.

I thanked him so much for what he did for my husband.

A girl asked me to follow her to ask me some questions. TC asked me to have Mark come back so he could talk to him.

I followed the girl to answer her questions and saw Mark and asked him if he could go back because TC wanted to talk to him.

I was returning to the emergency room to be with my husband when I noticed the paramedic, Ray, sitting behind the nurse's station. He looked up and asked me if I knew what happened?

 I told him yes, my husband told me.

I started to cry and put a hand over my heart and thanked him so much for bringing my husband back to life. Then I turned around and saw the other paramedic sitting in a chair and shook his hand, I couldn't thank them enough.

When I got back to TC, the cardiologist who was called in was with him. The cardiologist told me that they were taking my husband to surgery.

I started to cry and he told me that TC was at the right place and they were going to find out what was wrong with him.

As the rest of the Cardiac Team came in, my husband and I thanked them for coming.

I started to cry again. The doctor came over to me, gave me a hug. I told him I needed that.

As TC was rolled out, he told the nurses that he wanted me to come pray for him.

Through tears and shaking uncontrollably, I asked God to use the doctor and nurses' hands through this surgery to make my TC better than he was before, totally healing him in Jesus' name.

I stood there looking at the doctor and the nurses as they rolled my husband over to the other side of the doors where the operating room was.

I took a deep breath and said, "Oh Jesus, it is all in Your hands now." There was a peace that came over me as I thanked Jesus for His love, mercy and grace.

"You have never left me alone. You have always been there for me and I thank you," I said.

The doctor came back out and told me that the procedure would take up to two hours.

He would come out to let me know how things progressed and if they had to do more. I thanked him again.

I went back to the emergency room and told Mark that TC would be in surgery for at least two hours and asked, "Could you take me back home so I can get my car and come back?" I wanted Mark to get some rest before he had to go to work.

He said he was fine and, if I wanted to stay, he would stay with me. He was concerned about me driving back to the hospital. I told him I was fine. TC was in good hands.

When I got home, I greeted Lexus with hugs and kisses. She was looking for her daddy. I let her outside for a break while I took a shower, and got dressed. Then I loved on Lexus again.

I got in the car to drive and kept praying that TC would live and thanked Him for His healing power, in Jesus' name.

When I arrived back at the hospital, I was told that the doctor had come out to talk to me but I had just missed him.

I gasped for breath and asked her if I could go and find him behind the swinging doors where the operating room was.

She asked me to sit down and she would let me know when the doctor was ready for me.

"Oh Jesus, no," was all I could think to myself. I concluded that my husband did not make it through surgery.

I felt like I could not breath, move or anything. I was in total shock.

I said to myself, "Get it together. You trust God or you don't. And I sure do."

I asked God to forgive me and thanked Him for the work He had done on my husband's heart.

The lady at the desk asked me to come with her. She had me to sit on a stool and wait for the doctor.

My first reaction was my husband didn't make it through surgery. I prayed, "Oh God, I know you are going to help me through this one if he doesn't make it."

It was like the story of the footprints in the sand. God was carrying me through it all because He knew it was too much for me to handle.

The doctor came out and told me that TC's left ascending artery has closed up and that he had put in two stents and a balloon.

He said my husband was going into the Intensive Care Unit to be monitored and that it would be one day at a time.

I thanked God for letting my husband live and knew He had more work for TC to do.

It was such a beautiful sight to see my husband after he came out of surgery! I kissed him and thanked the nurses as we all walked up to the ICU.

They asked me to stay in the waiting room until they got him settled into his room.

After about 45 minutes, I saw a nurse come out of his room laughing, saying, "I can't believe he is joking around and making us laugh."

I looked up and said, "Thank you, Lord, and forgive me for not having enough faith."

I went into my husband's room, gave him a kiss and told him he had the nurses laughing with his jokes. I kept touching TC's arm and thanking God for letting him live.

On Monday, March 26, I wanted to find out the names of the heroes who had helped bring my husband back to life. I went to Fire Station No. 6, walked into the bay area and started to cry.

A fireman came up to me asking if I needed help and if I was all right.

I explained to him that I needed to know if this was the station that the crews of the ambulance and fire pickup truck came from who answered the call to our house – and brought my husband back to life.

He asked me to follow him into the station to talk to the lieutenant.

I asked the lieutenant the same question.

He asked me the date and time when I called 911.

I told him it was Tuesday, March 20, at around 1 to 2 AM.

I told him that there were two male paramedics; one of them was a big guy.

He asked me if he was tall. I said, "Really tall. Taller than you, but not as thin as you."

He asked if he had hair and I told him, "Yes, and I know you are bald." We both laughed and I needed that laugh.

He told me their names.

He said Ray the paramedic was here. "Would you like to talk to him?" I said, "Yes!"

We went into a hallway and entered a room where Ray was. I said, "Ray, you really are not that tall. I thought you were at least 7 feet tall." We all laughed.

I thanked him again for what he had done. He said he was just doing his job. I said, "No. You did more than your job and I will forever be grateful to you and everyone."

I thanked the lieutenant again and asked him to thank everyone else for me for all they had done.

After five days in ICU and two days in a regular room, I was able to bring my husband home!

Praise God. Thank You, Jesus!

The nurse told me what he could and could not do, so I had to have my husband on "lock down."

The nurse told me that he would go through different feelings and be very emotional at times because it was his heart, which made a lot of sense.

I told TC that he could listen or not but God gave him another chance here on earth so he better be grateful and do what he should do.

If you are lonely and hurting so badly that you feel you can't make it, believe me, you will not be able to come through it on your own. You are never alone, there is a man who walked this earth and went through a lot more that we could ever imagine going through and His name is Jesus.

The stripes He took on His back were for our healing (mind, body and heart). Whatever you need, call on the name of Jesus. He always hears you and always shows up right on time to help you.

When my thoughts are not right I put my hands on my head and plead the blood of Jesus over my mind to get my mind right.

Over my lifetime I have realized that you can't have a testimony without a test. Everything I have gone through in my life, God has used me to help someone else through what I have already experienced. The satisfaction of helping someone is indescribable.

We live by faith (substance of things hoped for and the evidence of things not seen) and not by sight.

God is in charge if you let Him, and He will be the driver if you let Him. I know I want Him to be in charge of my life. That is for sure!

What God has done for us, He will do for you. He is our Perfect Father and does not favor one over the other. Try Him and know that God is so good!

Isaiah 41:10
"Fear not (there is nothing to fear), for I am with you; do not look around you in terror and be dismayed, for I am your God. I will strengthen and hardened you to difficulties, yes, I will help; yes, I will hold you up and retain you with My (victorious) right hand of rightness and justice."

Whatever It Takes

When I first wrote my best selling real estate investing program, Vickie and I felt it was important to leave the people who bought that program with some encouraging words. We choose a little missive called, *"Whatever it Takes"*. No one knows who wrote these words but I heard that they were written by a Christian missionary who was about to be martyred for the cause of Christ in the morning and he wrote the following words the night before and placed them in his shoe. It made a HUGE impact on the students who purchased the program. We even had a testimonial, still on file, from a Pastor who was considering committing suicide until he bought our program and read *Whatever it Takes!*

WHATEVER IT TAKES

I am committed to doing "Whatever It Takes." I have Holy Spirit Power. The die has been cast. I've stepped over the line. I am out of the comfort zone. The decision has been made. I'm a disciple of His. I won't look back, let up, slow down or back away. My past is redeemed, my present makes sense and my future is secure. I am finished and done with low living, sight walking, small planning, smooth knees, colorless dreams, tame visions, mundane talking, tiny giving and dwarfed goals. I no longer need preeminence, prosperity, position, promotions or popularity. I don't have to be right, first, tips, recognized, praised, regarded or rewarded. I now learn by faith, love by patience, lift by prayer and labor by power. My face is set, my gait is fast, my goal is heaven, my road is narrow, my way is rough, my companions few, my Guide reliable and my mission clear. I cannot be bought, compromised, detoured, lured away, turned back, diluted or delayed. I will not flinch in the face of sacrifice, hesitate in the presence of adversity, negotiate at the table of the enemy, ponder at the pool of popularity, or meander in the maze of mediocrity. I won't give up, shut up or burn up-till I've preached up, prayed up, paid up, stored up and stayed up for the cause of Jesus Christ. I am a disciple of Jesus. I must go 'til I drop, preach 'til all know and work 'til He stops. I'm going to hang on, hunker down, hug tight and go where He wants to go and let Him take me there. And when He comes to get His own, He'll have no trouble recognizing me because I have committed my life to doing...

WHATEVER IT TAKES!

MAKE A DIFFERENCE TODAY!

One of the things that I have learned in my life is that what you help make happen in someone else's life God will help make happen for you and your life.

If you need a miracle in your own life then there is no faster way to your miracle than to help someone else who needs a miracle.

You will reap what you sow, no questions asked.

You now have the opportunity to share the "God Says When" message with so many who desperately need to hear this message and, by doing so, plant the seeds of a harvest in your own life.

I have seen firsthand folks' emotional reaction to this story.

So many people are hurting today, in every area, marriage, health, family and finances.

They feel like giving up and that there is no hope.

Right now, you could probably think of 5-10 people who need to hear the "God Says When" message.

You can be the conduit of someone's miracle!

It is so easy to do.

Simply email or call them and share the GodSaysWhen.com website.

If you are on Facebook post a link to GodSaysWhen.com and make sure you "Like" our Page on facebook.com/Godsayswhen

Share our website on Twitter.

Tell your Pastor about this book.

If you have a favorite columnist or reporter, Christian radio or TV show send them an email or call them telling them to visit the GodSaysWhen.com website.

Each time you do so you are planting a miracle seed in someone else's life.

That to me is quite exciting.

If you bought the book on Amazon.com, please make sure that you leave a review.

Amazon gives great weight to reviews and everyone helps.

It is important that you know that this book was written and published and available on Amazon.com within 3 months of my cardiac arrest.

3 months.

That is almost impossible to do, especially when recovering from a cardiac event. But I knew I was supposed to get this book out as soon as possible.

Plus, I really could not rest until this work was completed.

Writing this book has been so emotional.

The pages in this book are drenched with my tears as I relived the event.

I have followed the mandate I was given by the Lord in the ICU to the letter.

Scott Colley, my good friend, once told me, "TC, I do not want to be involved in any business that does not have the breath of God on it."

I have always remembered that.

I believe God's breath is on this book.

It will be read in all nations because of God touching people's hearts compelling them to share the "God Says When" message – like my friend, John Alexander, who said to me this is a message that must be shared and he intends to share it.

Or the TV reporter who with tears in her eyes after hearing my story said "Please let me know when the book is published and I will come back out and interview you again"

That is God's favor.

That is God's breath breathing on something.

I was very clear on the cover design as well.

It was to be a black cover with white letters, *God Says When!*

Not some fancy cover with clouds and graphics which I could have easily made.

Just three simple, powerful words that can change your life forever.

God Says When.

It is so simple for you to make a difference in someone's life just by sharing this message with someone via our website.

I will never forget my high school friend, Sue Wasielewski, who in the midst of her own battle for life, when she found out about my battle, uttered a prayer for me.

What you help make happen in someone else's life God will help make happen for you and your life.

You can be a conduit to someone's God Says When miracle just by sharing the GodSaysWhen.com website with an email, Facebook post, Twitter or phone call.

How cool is that!

Remember, as long as there is breath in your body and even when there is not breath in your body there is still HOPE!

I believe that you are here by divine appointment and for a reason.

It really is never too late for God to do a miracle in your life.

Never.

TC Bradley

"May the Lord bless you and keep you: May the Lord make His face shine upon you, and be gracious unto you: May the Lord lift up his countenance upon you and give you peace."

CONTACT INFORMATION

TC and Vickie Bradley are available to speak anywhere in the USA and Overseas.

For more information, please contact:

Mail:

TC and Vickie Bradley
New Life Vision, LLC
1616 W. Cape Coral Parkway #231
Cape Coral, Florida

Website:

GodSaysWhen.com

Facebook.com/GodSaysWhen

Email: Info@GodSaysWhen.com

Phone: (239) 549-9868

Made in the USA
Middletown, DE
11 December 2021

55176033R00046